Going, Going, Gone?

Written by James Talia

Series Consultant: Linda Hoyt

WorldWise™
Content-based Learning

Contents

Introduction

The huge dinosaurs that once roamed the earth fascinate us. These reptiles ruled the land, the skies and the seas, but they no longer exist. They are now **extinct**.

The same thing could happen to our largest land animal, the elephant. Or to tigers, polar bears and orangutans.

Many **species** of animals like these are now **endangered**, and could one day soon become extinct.

An artist's impression of dinosaurs that once roamed the earth.

	Guam kingfisher	White-collared lemur
Risk rating	Extinct in the wild	Critically endangered
How serious	Extreme risk	

panese red-crowned crane	American bison	Red howler monkey
Endangered	**Near threatened**	**Least concern**

Low risk

Chapter 1

Why do animals become extinct?

On our planet, it is quite normal for animals to become **extinct**. This has been happening for millions of years. Fossils found in rocks and soil tell us this. Fossils are the bones and remains of animals that no longer live on the earth.

Why have so many animals become extinct?

One reason is the big changes to the environment of the earth. In the past, sometimes the earth has been much warmer and at other times much colder than today. As the environment has changed, whole **species** of animals have died.

Animals compete with each other for food and shelter. When the **climate** gets much colder or hotter, plants change and die. Then animals need to feed on different food, and some do not survive.

The woolly mammoth is extinct.

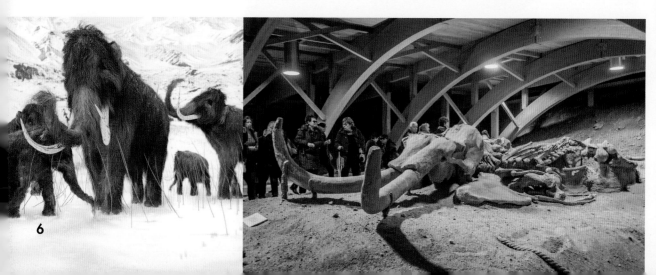

Humans and the environment

Should we be worried about animals becoming extinct today?

We compete with other animals for food, shelter and the many other things that we use to live our lives. As the **population** increases, we use more and more of Earth's **resources**. This damages the environment and destroys the **habitat** of many animals.

Humans **encroach** on the habitat of animals

How people today change the environment

Agriculture

Human activity

- Clearing land to grow food crops and grain for animals
- Clearing and fencing land to raise farm animals

Effect on native plants and animals

- Habitat is destroyed.
- **Predators** or pests are shot, trapped or poisoned.

Industry

Human activity

- Cutting down trees for firewood
- Cutting down trees to make paper
- Building factories that cause pollution

Effect on native plants and animals

- Habitat is destroyed.
- Animals that cannot move or **adapt** become extinct.

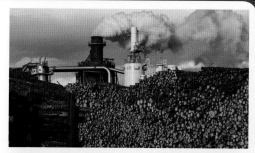

Cities and towns

Human activity

- Building cities, freeways, roads, railroads

Effect on native plants and animals

- Habitat is destroyed.
- Native plants and animals are removed.
- Animals that cannot move or adapt become extinct.

Building on wetlands, mangroves and beaches

Human activity

- Building houses, resorts, golf courses and entertainment centres

Effect on native plants and animals

- Habitat is destroyed.
- Animals that cannot move or adapt become extinct.

Chapter 2
Animals with uncertain futures

Around the world, there are some animal **species** that are in serious danger of soon becoming **extinct**. Many actions are being taken by people to try to save them, but their futures remain uncertain.

Tasmanian devils

Sometimes an animal species can become threatened because of a serious disease that spreads through the groups. A kind of cancer that grows on their faces is killing Tasmanian devils. Eventually the lumps and sores prevent the animals from feeding, and this results in death. Devils are noisy and squabble among themselves when feeding. Their biting and aggressive behaviour around food may be spreading this disease.

Find out more

You might be interested in finding the places where Tasmanian devils are healthy and living without any sign of cancer. Some of these animals are in Australian and international zoos and others in wildlife **refuges**. There are also some healthy **populations** in the wild. Watch for stories about the **vaccine**.

Tasmanian devils are now **endangered**. Once, they lived widely throughout Australia, but now devils are only found in the wild in Tasmania.

They are very striking, strong, muscular animals about the size of a small dog. They prey on smaller **native** animals, birds and reptiles. They also eat dead animals, fruit and vegetable material.

Tasmanian devil numbers are falling quickly. Their numbers can fall to a very low level until there are no healthy animals that can breed with each other.

What can be done?

It is hoped that a vaccine to prevent or cure the disease will be found. At the moment, separating healthy animals away from diseased animals helps Tasmanian devils to survive.

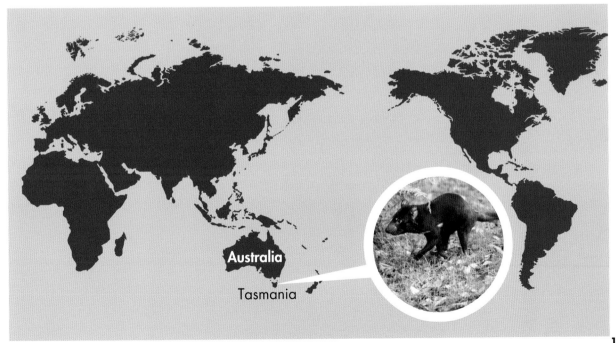

Australia

Tasmania

Amur leopards

Amur leopards live in a cold, snowy climate in small areas of Russia and China. They are well suited to living there. They have hairy coats that grow thicker in the winter to keep them warm. Their long legs enable them to move in deep snow.

But Amur leopards are critically endangered because less than 60 of these animals survive in their natural habitat.

Amur leopard in the snow

People are taking over the habitat of the leopards. They hunt deer, wild pigs and moose that are the prey of the leopards. The leopards have had to find other food to eat. They now hunt the animals in deer farms, and some are killed by farmers protecting their deer.

A mother with her cub in a zoo

People in Russia, China and other countries are trying to save the Amur leopards from extinction. It is illegal to kill these animals, or to sell their skins. Burning or cutting down forests has been stopped. Zoos are helping their survival by breeding them. By 2011, there were 173 Amur leopards in zoos around the world.

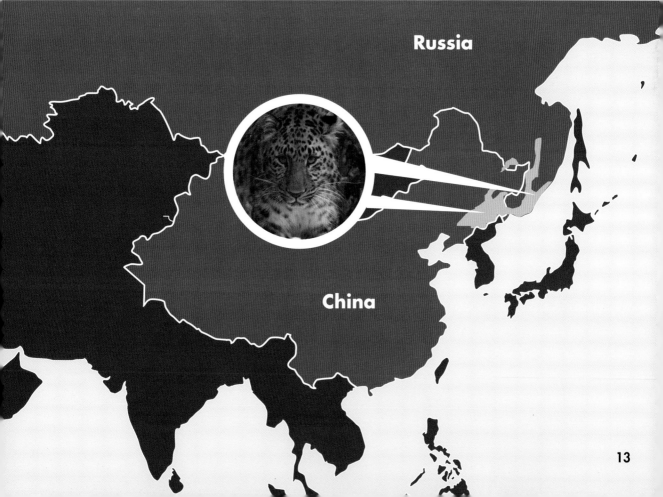

Polar bears

Polar bears are only found in the Arctic Circle. Their bodies are well adapted to cold temperatures, and they can move across ice, snow and through very cold water.

The main food for this large **predator** is seals. Seals swim much faster than polar bears, so they are rarely caught by the bears in the water. But seals like to come out of the water to rest on the sea ice. When they sense danger, they quickly move back to the safety of the water.

During spring, before the sea ice melts, the bears are able to catch the seals.

Mother polar bear and cub walking on Arctic ice.

This season is their main chance to build up the body fat they have lost during the long winter **hibernation** when they cannot feed.

But the earth is getting warmer. The sea ice now melts earlier in the spring and freezes again later in autumn. The seal-hunting season is much shorter and this is threatening the survival of these magnificent bears.

Without sea ice, food is very scarce in the summer. Many bears will starve before the sea freezes and they can hunt seals again. Females cannot raise healthy cubs without enough body fat. Their need for food brings more bears into contact with humans, which is often dangerous for the bears and sometimes for the humans.

What can be done?

Stopping or at least slowing the increase in the earth's temperature is the only action likely to help the polar bear to survive.

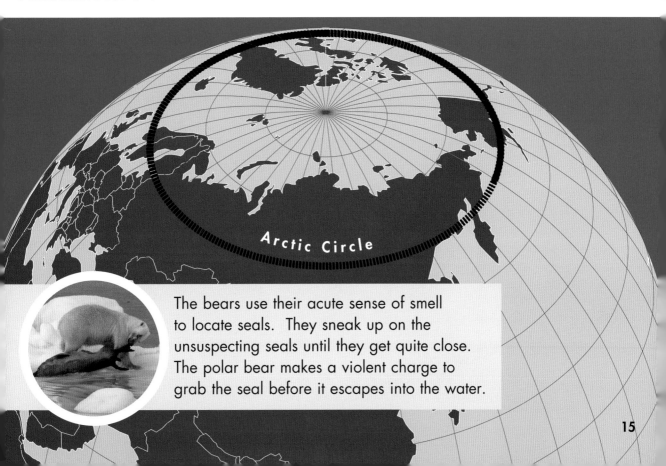

Arctic Circle

The bears use their acute sense of smell to locate seals. They sneak up on the unsuspecting seals until they get quite close. The polar bear makes a violent charge to grab the seal before it escapes into the water.

Chapter 3

The good news: Success stories

Some groups of people have succeeded in saving animal **species** that were in serious danger of soon becoming **extinct**.

Whooping cranes

These birds are about 1.5 metres tall and are the tallest North American bird. They were once found throughout midwestern North America and spent the winter in the warmer southern states by the Gulf of Mexico. Whooping cranes have always been a rare species. The **population** was believed to be around 10,000 birds before Europeans arrived in North America.

Whooping cranes run before takeoff

Whooping cranes are prey to large animals such as bears, wolves, mountain lions and bald eagles. From the mid-1800s to mid-1900s, their feathers became popular decorations for women's hats. This and the loss of **habitat** to farming and other uses of the wetlands where they live resulted in only one population left in the wild.

In 1941, the wild population of whooping cranes was just 16 birds. The actions of many people led to their summer breeding areas in Alberta, Canada, and in Wisconsin, the United States, being protected. The birds were declared endangered in 1967. Groups began to successfully breed birds in **captivity**. Many have been released back into the wild.

By 2012, the wild population had grown to about 382, with another 152 living in captivity. This graceful species is still on the **endangered** list, but has a much healthier population today.

Rising numbers of whooping cranes are a success story.

Whale recovery

Whales, the largest animals that ever lived on the earth, were hunted by humans for 300 years. Whale products such as cooking oil, candles and soap were important in people's lives.

At first, hunters on whaling ships powered by sails used hand-thrown harpoons to kill hundreds of thousands of sperm whales. In the 20th century, diesel engines and exploding **harpoons** were used, making it easier to kill whales. Almost three million whales of all species were killed.

These huge animals live long lives and are not able to breed until they are around ten years of age. Females have a calf every two to five years, so populations of whales do not recover quickly. Whaling was banned in 1996, but some countries do not accept this decision and some whales continue to be killed each year.

A whaling ship (top); a humpback whale

Today, there is growing interest in whale watching. The more people know about whales, the more they will take an interest in their future and become involved with groups that try to protect whales.

Tourists on the boat are whale watching.

Whaling greatly reduced the numbers of great whales; many are endangered

Species

Grey whale		
Population before whaling	**20,000**	
Population after whaling	**20,000**	
Status	least concern	

Humpback whale		
Population before whaling	**100,000**	
Population after whaling	**60,000**	
Status	low concern	

Blue whale		
Population before whaling	**175,000**	
Population after whaling	**10,000⁺**	
Status	endangered	

Find out more

Which countries continued killing whales after 1996? Which whales can be seen off the coast of your country?

Which other animals are critically endangered?

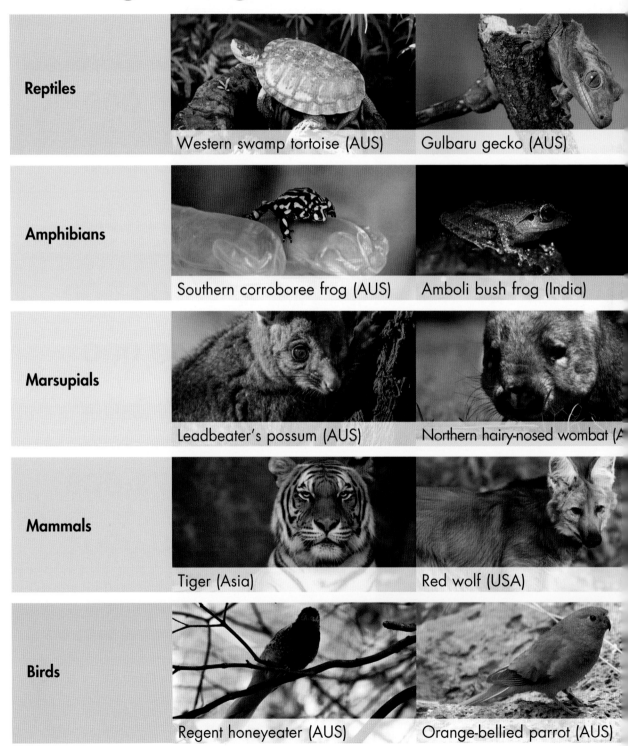

Reptiles	Western swamp tortoise (AUS)	Gulbaru gecko (AUS)
Amphibians	Southern corroboree frog (AUS)	Amboli bush frog (India)
Marsupials	Leadbeater's possum (AUS)	Northern hairy-nosed wombat (A
Mammals	Tiger (Asia)	Red wolf (USA)
Birds	Regent honeyeater (AUS)	Orange-bellied parrot (AUS)

Kemp's ridley sea turtle (USA)

Gharial (India)

Lemur tree frog (Panama)

Montseny brook newt (Spain)

Gilbert's potoroo (AUS)

Golden-mantled tree-kangaroo (New Guinea)

Florida bonnet bat (USA)

Western gorilla (Africa)

Californian condor (USA)

Waved albatross (Galápagos)

Conclusion

There is nothing new about animals becoming **extinct**. Their survival is affected by changes to the earth over very long periods of time. The **climate** changes, the seas change, the surface of the earth changes and the plants growing also change.

Animals change very slightly over very long periods of time, and the ones that are better able to survive continue to live, and those that cannot become extinct.

Of all living things, humans are the most successful species that have ever lived on Earth. Humans used tools and invented machines that have enabled them to clear land and destroy **habitats** that are home to many animal **species**. Human activity is the reason why so many more animals are facing extinction today. Many people are aware of this and are doing different things to save animals from extinction.

Glossary

adapt to change in ways that suit new conditions

captivity the state of being in a place such as a zoo, where living things are not living in the wild

climate the average or usual weather conditions in a place

encroach to move or go into an area outside the usual limits

endangered at a high risk of dying out and becoming extinct

extinct when a group of living things no longer has any living members left

habitat the place where a plant or an animal naturally lives

harpoons spears with pointy, sharp, hooked tips, usually used to hunt sea animals

hibernation to become inactive throughout winter, by slowing down body systems

native a living thing that originated, and has always lived in a particular place

population/s the total number of a certain group of living things

predator/s animals that get food by killing and eating other animals

refuges places that provide protection

resources things found in nature that are valuable and helpful to people, particularly in providing energy

species a group of living things that are alike in many ways, have many traits in common and are able to have offspring

vaccine a substance that is given to provide protection from a particular disease

Index